# Office Politics

# ...The Right Way:

## 7 Principles to Create Win-Win Relationships in the Workplace

# Edward L. Jones

Coach | Author | Speaker

Office Politics the Right Way: 7 Principles to Create Win-Win Relationships in the Workplace

Cover produced by Angela Lofton Moore – InfoPrincess

Editing by Deanna Vestal

Published in the United States of America

Sunshine Solutions Publishing
9912 Business Park Dr., Ste. 170
Sacramento, CA 95827


Library of Congress Control Number   2019909453

ISBN-13: 9781079799255

# Acknowledgements

I thank Tiana Von Johnson my branding coach for challenging me to write a book. Without her I never would have done it. She was instrumental in helping to select the initial book cover design also. My daughter, Iman, and wife, Gloria, provided valuable editorial insight and perspective which helped me consider the world of work from different perspectives. Floyd Hoelting, my former boss and mentor, saw something in me that I didn't. He challenged and supported me throughout my career. My WorkFlow Lounge family are helping me shape a new career as an entrepreneur. A special shout out to Phillis Clements for guiding me through the publishing process. Most importantly I thank God. Without Him I would not be here to tell the story.

# Introduction

When I mention the words "Office Politics" most people cringe. It uncovers thoughts of unpleasant memories or highlights a current situation. Almost everyone has a story about a boss, colleague, or subordinate.

*Office Politics the Right Way* flips the script by sharing approaches that create win-win-win office relationships. A win for supervisors, colleagues, and subordinates.

Office politics is present in all types of organizations and it can affect the population it serves. Whether they are called clients, customers, patients, students or parishioners, an organization's mission is to serve them well. Without them the organization cannot grow or even survive long term.

Office politics is like money and time. It has value but is neither good or bad. What matters is how it is used. Humans consciously choose to use it for good or evil. In some cases, they unwittingly leave it to fate.

Fate can be cruel. So rather than letting fate be the master of your organization, take control, by using office politics in a manner that best serves the organization. Unchecked and unbridled office politics can destroy an organization.

Communication is the glue that holds all relationships together. It is one of the underlying pillars of mastering office politics the right way. Everyone seems to know that, but it is much easier said than done, especially in fast paced offices.

Words mean different things to different people. Even if the words are interpreted correctly, tone and body language can create misunderstandings. I've been employing an approach that takes time on the front end but saves time in the long run when engaged in intense or volatile conversations. First, I make eye contact, then I listen to the words, I feel the tone, and observe the body language. All provide clues that determine what the individual is saying and/or not saying. After listening, I pause to make sure they have finished. I paraphrase so they know they were heard and then I respond.

Stephen Covey, in *The 7 Habits of Highly Effective People*, states that slow is fast when dealing with people. If a conversation is misunderstood, it takes time to repair a relationship, redirect a program or the project. Slower communication gives individuals the best chance to get it right the first time.

A few years ago, my wife and I had a low-cost miscommunication, but this example stayed with me. I called her to pick me up at the doctor's office. I asked if she knew where it was; she said, "yes." An hour later I was still waiting for her. She was at a different office waiting for me. The doctor had two office locations. The doctor; one near where we used to live and one near to where we had recently moved. A half hour later she picked me up. We talked it out and we laugh about it now. Rather than saying, "do you know where it is?" I should have said, "there is a location near our new address." You live and learn.

Another factor that provides a foundation for conducting office politics the right way is trust. It too provides a stabilizing force to all relationships. Trust makes communication easier. Misinterpretations are less likely when there is trust.

Honesty and integrity are the primary elements of trust. I often say, "it's not what you want to hear, but it's what you need to hear that makes anyone better", especially leaders. I am probably not the first to say it, and I certainly won't be the last.

Those who surround themselves with "yes people" do so at their own peril. One of my managers and I had very little in common, but we trusted each other because our word was our bond. When I asked for something by a certain date, the information was delivered on or before the due date and often exceeded my expectations. When I made a promise, I kept it. He was not a "yes man" and we didn't always agree, but, we respected each other's opinions and positions in the organization. I often told him that if I was going to battle and could only take one person, it would be him.

Brene' Brown brought up vulnerability as a component of trust building in her book, *Dare to Lead*. That was something I hadn't considered. It includes building relationships by sharing fears, flaws, and other shortcomings with people in the work place. This deeply personal information can't be shared with everyone however. It takes a great deal of discernment to determine who can be trusted with such information.

Bottomline, communication and trust go hand in hand. One must actively listen to determine who s/he can trust and how much. Trust and communication in organizations are as important to an organization's success as air, water, and food are to the body; it is difficult to survive without them.

# Table of Contents

# Section I

# Principle 1: Self-Awareness

## *The Mirror*

I have listened to, and even engaged in conversations about what is going wrong in an organization. Many people have an opinion about how someone else could do a job or relate to others better.

After graduating with my first master's degree, I was hired as a Resident Counselor at the University of Cincinnati. That was back in the day when "I knew it all". Warren Bennis, one of the best-known leadership gurus at the time, was President of the University. I had had a great year according to my standards. During a dinner outing I bragged to my then girlfriend, now my wife, that if the Director left, I'd be the Director, and if the Dean of Students left, the obvious choice to replace him was me. Then I set my sights even higher. Could you imagine, if Warren Bennis was to leave, the new President would be me? Well as it turns out, all of them were terminated in a massive reorganization. I could feel the blade of the board's ax cut an inch off my afro. Yes, you guessed it, I did not become the Director, Dean, or President. I was happy to still have a job. The point of this story is this: I had a distorted view of my value and contribution to the organization.

With all that being said, accurate self-analysis is very important. As the great playwright and poet Shakespeare wrote; "To thine own self be true, then you cannot be false to any man". My pseudo self-esteem had to be replaced by the real thing, an accurate reflection of myself.

When I was an undergraduate, I worked for a renowned professional trainer, but I didn't pay close attention to the educational leadership principles he taught. Remember, those were the days when I thought I knew it all. A few years later, I paid to learn what I could have learned from him at no cost had I been more self-aware.

There is a systematic way to break down human interaction and perceptions that are frequently used in management. It is called the Johari Window. The Johari Window is an exercise that helps people better understand themselves and others. It was developed by psychologists Joseph Luft and Harrington Ingham. It is used primarily in educational and corporate settings to help teams learn to understand each other better through feedback and disclosure. The better we know ourselves the better we can present a true reflection of who we are to others.

See the graphic depicting the Johari Window on the next page.

There is one simple question that can determine how self-aware a person is. "Who are you?" Some say personality is formed by external forces, however I believe some things are innate. Eileen Donahue and Keith Harary put it this way, "when your inner nature meets lived experiences you begin to know who you are." Seeing yourself through others' eyes is important.

Outside forces contribute, but you are in the driver's seat.

Here are examples of how outside forces contribute. Have you ever dressed in a hurry, left for work, and forgotten to look in the mirror? Someone else would have to tell you if something was out of place. At least you hope someone would. No supportive coworker or friend would allow you to walk around all day with toilet paper on your shoe. Certainly you would welcome that feedback. On the other hand, there are probably times when you have had sleepless nights that have caused lethargic days at work. Coworkers could easily attribute your silence or aloofness to some discontent you have with them unless you disclose the reason for your more reserved demeanor. Feedback and disclosure are the cornerstones of the Johari Window. What could you learn about yourself by participating in a Johari Window exercise with co-workers?

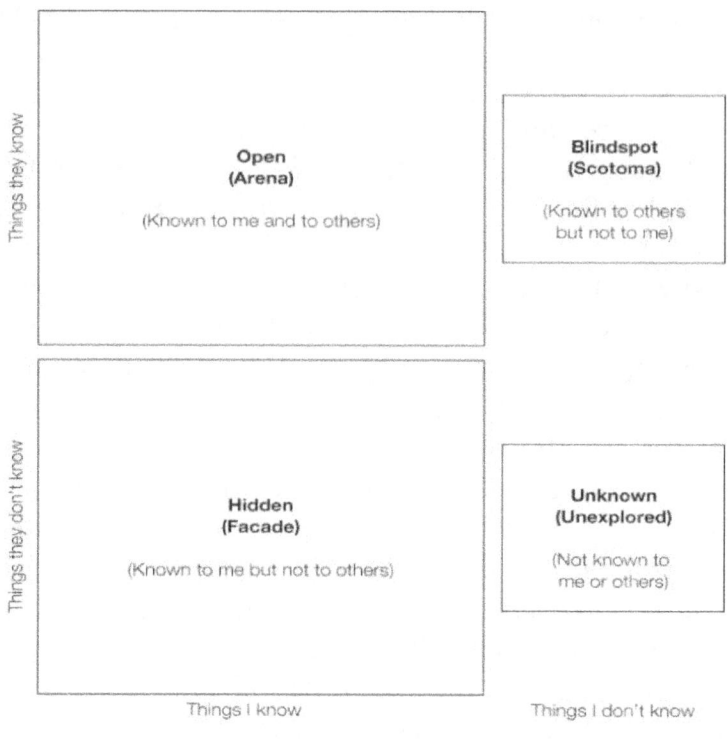

The Johari Window

## *Self-Talk*

Is the glass half empty or half full? Is it partly sunny or partly cloudy? In both cases the conditions are the same. What is different is what we tell ourselves, our self-talk. Some people call self-talk the inner game. These are things that you think, but don't say out loud. When you meet a person for the first time, you might make judgements about them. But do your thoughts reflect more about you than them?

Henry Ford said, "Whether you think you can, or you think you can't, you're right." How you talk to yourself can determine how you engage others and how you behave in social settings. Positive self-talk makes you feel good about yourself, the people and things around you. It's an optimistic voice in your head that always looks on the bright side. Negative self-talk does the opposite, draining mental and physical energy. The fruit of self-talk is expressed in the following poem.

### The Man Who Thinks He Can

If you think you are beaten, you are;
If you think you dare not, you don't
If you'd like to win, but think you can't
It is almost  cinch you won't.
If you think you'll lose, you've lost,
For out in the world we find
Success begins with a fellow's will;
It's all in the state of mind

If you think you're out classed, you are:
You've got to think high to rise.
You've got to be sure of yourself  before
You can ever win the prize
Life's battles don't always go
To the stronger or faster man,
But soon or late the man who wins
Is the one who thinks he can.

I know that bad situations exist in the workplace and elsewhere, so I am not suggesting that you go through life with child-like naiveté. Using positive self-talk can help you make the best out of a bad situation. Think long term. Opportunities may not be available today but staying positive will get you noticed by those who are looking for positive people to work in their organizations.

I met a person who worked in a very dysfunctional organization. Morale was low and the overall performance of the department was in a downward spiral. Several employees were gossiping and working half heartily. But this person did not gossip and continued to perform well. That person was a red apple in a barrel of green ones. Within a short period of time, she was hired by a high performing organization.

Tiffany Haddish, comedian/actress, had a rough childhood. Through it all, she kept a positive outlook on life. I don't know if her positive self-talk was innate or if she learned over time, but it made a positive difference in her life and career.

Self-talk can be based on experiences from the past or pre-judgments. The good news is anyone can learn positive self-talk. If the feelings are negative, ask yourself where they are coming from. I learned a lot about myself from the Harley-Davidson experience that I will share later.

You can change a glass half empty to a glass half full mindset, if you choose to. The prescription is easy, but the application can be hard. Having a plan and practicing is the key. You can change your outlook a bit easier, if you practice meditation and affirmations.

Once again, the first thing you must do is choose to engage in positive self-talk. GratitudeHabitat.com offered the following when working with others:

1.    Think before you speak.

2.    Is it true?

3.    Are my words helpful?

4.    Are my words necessary?

5.    Are my words kind?

6.    Are my words encouraging?

I suggest you use this same criteria for self-talk.


## *Centered*

Self-knowledge leads to positive self-talk which will help you become grounded and centered as a leader. According to Katie Hoban, "Being centered in yourself means that your thoughts, ideas, actions, and conversations revolve around things other than yourself, but draw strength from within instead of from others." Carol Robin put it this way, "Being centered means that you have a reference point or a place to come back to when life's challenges and emotions push you off balance. The center is the place you know you must get back to. Your character, values and purpose comprise your center."

It is important to be emotionally centered, not self-centered. A self-centered person is exclusively concerned about what's in it for them while an emotionally centered person is concerned about others and the purpose of the organization.

Most people understand the value of being emotionally centered in the workplace. Considering the long-term benefits, leaders should want to manage in a way that promotes positive relationships and produces high quality products and services. But in a fast-paced environment, it can be easy to get off track. Schedules must be kept and money must be made. When there is so much to do and so little time, we need to press pause for a moment.

I consider myself to be self-aware, empathetic with an abundance of social skills, but there were times when I felt the need to be expedient. In times of crisis, this is often necessary. But, I had to make sure to circle back for damage control. I ran across a Facebook meme that reads as follows: "Four things you can't recover: The stone after the throw, the word after it's said, the occasion after it's missed, and time after it is gone."

Even in a crisis it is important to be grounded and centered in your character, values, and purpose. Similarly, to positive self-talk, it takes practice. When things are going well it is so easy to extol the virtues of being centered. However, during trying times the 'real you' will surface. Unless you are mindful of what it takes to be centered, words you don't recognize could come out of your mouth.

Here are some things to consider. When an emotional rush comes due to an unexpected situation, pause and take a deep breath, collect your thoughts, and choose your words carefully. You may not be able to control your tone and body language but do the best you can. In unpleasant and stressful times, you want to remain centered.

Journaling and meditation are tools that can be used to keep you calm and centered. Self-talk and reflection can also be useful. It is best to be mindful, but if things go wrong think about what could have been done differently and be ready to try new options should a similar situation arise. It is all based on your center. Know where it is and use it as an anchor to be most effective.

# Principle 2: Dynamics of Leadership

## *Organization Culture*

As an executive, being armed with self-knowledge and the tools to operate effectively were very important to me. I developed the appropriate mindset, skills, and abilities to address various situations in the workplace. Everything I've learned about self-management was in preparation for dealing with organization, culture, and climate. Yes, there is a difference. Organization culture (macro) has a broad focus and is not as obvious to those within the organization. It is what I have often referred to as an organization's external personality. Organization climate (micro) is narrowly focused on specific areas such as interpersonal engagement, attitudes, or diversity issues. Those within the organization are more aware of it. When the work environment is not quite up to par, they are often surveyed to get employee perceptions about them.

Organization culture and climate are not mutually exclusive. One impacts the other. A study on organizational climate and culture provided insight into the role an organization's environment has on its employees and organizational effectiveness. In other words, organizational culture and climate (positive or negative) are explicitly promoted or implicitly condoned from the top.

Organization leaders implement policies and procedures to meet their own goals, thereby creating strategic climates within their organizations. Their practices reflect their own values. Those values become enacted through the behaviors displayed by leadership teams in the organization, thereby operationalizing the core values that collectively define an organizations culture.

According to Organizational Culture Assessment Instrument (OCAI) online, "Competing Values Framework", there are 4 organizational cultures. I thought it helpful to review them to determine which one fit my style. I describe them here to help you do the same. They are Clan, Adhocracy, Market and Hierarchy.

## Clan

Clan culture is a friendly work environment. People have a lot in common and it's like a large family. The leaders are mentors or maybe even father/mother figures. The organization is held together by loyalty and tradition. The organization emphasizes long-term human resource development and bonds colleagues by morals. Success is defined within the framework of addressing the needs of the clients and caring for people. The organization promotes teamwork, participation, and consensus.

## Adhocracy

Adhocracy culture is a dynamic and creative work environment. Leaders and employees are encouraged to take calculated risks. Leaders are seen as innovators. Experimentation and innovation are the bonding materials within the organization. The long-term goal is to grow and create new resources. The availability of new products or services arc seen as success. The organization promotes individual initiatives and freedom.

## Marketing

Marketing culture is a results-based organization. People are competitive and focused on goals. Leaders are hard drivers, producers, and rivals at the same time. They are tough and have high expectations. The emphasis on winning keeps the organization together. Reputation and success are most important. The long-term focus is on activities and reaching goals. Market share is the definition of success. Competitive pricing and market leadership are also important.

## Hierarchy

Hierarchy culture is a formalized and structured work environment. Procedures decide what people do. Leaders are proud of their efficiency-based coordination and organization. Keeping the organization functioning smoothly is most crucial. Formal rules and policies keep the organization together. Long-term goals are stability and results, paired with efficient and smooth execution of tasks. Management's focus is on guaranteeing work and productivity.

It is paramount that leaders on lower rungs of the organization's ladder learn their organization's dominant culture to effectively manage up and down from the middle.

I learned how to manage up as a means of survival. I worked for a very inspirational, innovative, and demanding boss. He could think of innovative projects much faster than the staff in the department could implement them. I had the largest operation in the department. I had to manage my area as well as implement new projects and programs. One day he came to me with another exciting idea. However, I knew I couldn't take on anything without letting something else go. I showed him the timeline for each project and to whom I had delegated portions of it. I asked which project he'd like to delay so the new one could be done. He decided to hold off on the new project.

I had a great relationship with him because we had become friends, but I also understood he was the boss. I respected him as well as his position. He allowed me to speak freely with him. I knew I could give my honest opinion, even vehemently, and respectfully disagree without fear of losing my job. When you are not in a union you serve at the pleasure. At the end of the day I understood that my decisions were recommendations to him; it could go one of three ways: accepted whole, in part, or not at all. No matter what, he always gave me my "day in court". I describe his organization as a combination of Adhocracy and Clan. Upon reflection, I adopted the same approach when I became an executive leader.

## Proactive Leadership

Doris Day was a popular recording artist in the 50's and 60's. "Que sera sera whatever will be. The future is not ours to see que sera sera" were the lyrics to one of her hit songs. I liked the song but didn't like working in an organization with that management approach. Years ago, a colleague asked why I spent so much time planning. In his opinion, crises occur and Murphy's Law is always in play. So there is no reason to have a plan C. While that approach may work well for those adventurous souls who enjoy flying by the seat of their pants, I am more comfortable with a carefully planned agenda and clearly set goals. One of the first maxims I remember is, those who fail to plan, plan to fail.

That organization did not consciously plan to fail. It is still operating now, but the leadership changed frequently. It was a learning experience for me; I learned the importance of planning and became a proactive leader who anticipated potential obstacles and opportunities.

I am convinced that the organization described above consistently operated in crises mode because the culture did not support pro-action. Some people enjoy putting out fires but living from crisis to crisis was not my idea of fun. I knew there was a better way. I picked up a copy of Stephen Covey's, *The 7 Habits of Highly Effective People*. He used the word "proactive" before it was officially recognized by dictionaries. I found the Time Management Matrix most helpful. The title of the matrix is a misnomer, because it shows how to manage oneself, not time.

The matrix is divided into quadrants. Quadrant I contains tasks/issues that are important and urgent; a crisis, for example. Quadrant II is filled with items that are not urgent, but important; staff development and strategic planning, to name a few. Quadrant III consists of items that are not important, but urgent: such as answering telemarketing calls or responding to gossip on Facebook. Quadrant IV is where items that are neither important or urgent are housed; like entertainment television. Engaging in Quadrants I, III or IV have their places, but those activities may not give you the best chance for the best outcome in terms adhering to the organization's missions. I incorporated this 7 Habits approach into my life and put more emphasis on Quadrant II and became more proactive.

Creating a Marketing and Public Information unit was not urgent, but important because my department got a lot of media coverage. Collaborating with the Provost and Deans to develop Academic initiatives was not urgent, but important in terms of living-learning communities. Building a $26,000,000 state-of-the-art apartment complex was not urgent, but important to the future of a housing program with aging facilities.

Each of those projects took five years to plan and implement. The day-to-day issues didn't go away, but we always made time for what was most important. As far as day-to-day operations were concerned, I made a point to get to work early most days. I felt that by getting to work before others, I could survey the issues of the day and delegate them to the right people. In other words, if I got to work early, I could pitch, but if I got there later, I'd be stuck in crises mode attempting to catch up.

My mentor taught me an approach to use when delegating called "completed staff work." When a problem arose, he'd often say, "Don't bring me questions, bring me answers." I adopted his approach to problem solving and added a Socratic questioning technique for my direct reports to use when making decisions.

I told them there are few perfect decisions because we seldom have perfect information. The first thing I wanted them to do was to brainstorm possible solutions, then evaluate the upside and downside of each. Usually the option with the greatest upside and lowest downside was the best decision. Even if the decision didn't work out, we could review the thought process and learn from the experience.

Proactivity is not only about anticipating the future, it's about shaping it. It's about being able to choose our responses to external stimuli which will give us the best chance for this desired outcome and to become the master of our fate; not a victim of it.

## *Lateral Communication*

While most of my focus was on vertical integration (supervisor-subordinate relationships), lateral relationships with peers cannot be ignored. One of the biggest challenges of my career was the call to change the culture of a static department. Any change in one's professional life is a major adjustment, but the job of turning around a group of people who are content with their method of operation is daunting. They did not want to change. The department had a rigid bureaucratic culture with a reputation for dubious customer service.

Three of my five direct reports had applied for the position and one retired. Matters got worse when the person who hired me took another position in another state. The environment was very hostile. This was quite a contrast to my previous workplace, where I had a lot of political capital inside and out of the department. Now, here I was starting all over again, faced with a great challenge and opportunity to step out of my comfort zone and make a positive difference in the lives of others.

I was not certain who my allies were in the organization, I knew I had to build trust. I made it a point to speak with employees and customers. I wanted them to know me personally rather than rely on the opinions of others. In addition to those in the organization, I met with colleagues outside the department who were very supportive. Those relationships were helpful in terms of my survival, they were also good for the division.

Interdepartmental collaboration helped open the lines of communication between department heads and their respective staffs. The culture and reputation of the department I led was enhanced as a result.

After the organization's cultural adjustment, my focus shifted to refining lateral communication among the units within the department. Our collective vision and mission were clear, but employees were used to top down command and control vertical communication. Unit heads were more comfortable communicating directly with me than with each other.

Each unit felt it was the most important one in the department when in fact, all of them contributed equally. Through a series of working meetings, we collectively determined that lateral communication among units better served the interests of everyone. It made our department more efficient and effective.

# Principle 3: Empowering People

## *Set the Temperature*

Whether leaders recognize it or not, they set the tone for the organization they lead. I call it, "setting the temperature." During a "Lunch and Learn" I introduced myself and my coaching emphasis. After describing my role as a life coach, specializing in "Office Politics", many of the participants shared stories about their experiences with workplace situations. The person who owns the shared office space where I am a member told me she left her corporate position because of the tone her boss set.

She worked with a team of seven innovative colleagues who worked for a command and control manager with limited human relations skill. She was the second to the last team member to leave. Upper management finally caught on after losing six of seven excellent people.

Another entrepreneur announced that she knew four employees at two financial institutions who were experiencing frigid at best and hostile at worst work environments and considered other opportunities. Employees don't leave companies, they leave bad bosses.

A bad manager can take good staff and destroy them, causing the best employees to flee and the remainder to lose all motivation. Research shows that people with bad bosses are 60% more likely to have health issues than those with a good boss.

According to Brigette Hyacinth, there are four types of bosses: Marionette, King Kong, Superman, and Task-Master. The Marionette is typically a nice person who gets along with employees and supervisors. However, when the going gets tough they will allow their staff to be sacrificed with little or no resistance. They rarely push innovative boundaries with new ideas. They are more likely to wait to be told what to do then pass it down their chain of command, hoping to survive by being a "yes person." The King Kong style manager believes that he or she has privileges and power so they love to flaunt it. In some cases, they mask fears and flaws by intimidating subordinates considered threats to their authority. Managers who fall in the Superman style, operate as if nothing worthy of note could occur without them. They make decisions with little input from their employees and take credit for what is produced. The Task Master has high expectations for him/herself and those who work for them. They delegate projects then micromanage and push subordinates to meet tight deadlines on a regular basis.

If you know a boss who operates like the four described above or if you looked in the mirror and recognized some of those tendencies in yourself, there is hope. Although I had many strengths as a manager under duress, I tried to be Superman. I thank heaven for a wonderful staff and family who kept me grounded.

I found this meme posted by Johnnie L Campbell, "A truly great boss is hard to find, difficult to part with and impossible to forget." Isn't that someone you'd want to work for or how you'd want to be remembered?

According to Jacob Morgan, truly great managers act like coaches, focus on strengths, shore up weaknesses, get to know employees, embrace vulnerability, and challenge the status quo. They are interested in developing and supporting the whole person, not just a worker.

All managers are not leaders. On the other hand, one does not have to be a manager to lead. But when you find a manager who is a leader, employees are happy and productive.

Brene' Brown, author of *Dare to Lead*, puts it this way, "Leadership is not about titles, status and wielding power. A leader is anyone who takes responsibility for recognizing the potential in people and ideas and has the courage to develop that potential." Brigitte Hyacinth makes the point, " Employees want managers who are leaders. Managers who will inspire them, who are fair, honest, and will stand up for their team."

Skill and intellect are employee assets. The better the corporations, educational institutions, and non-profits enhance those assets, the better it will be for those organizations and the populations they serve.

## *Expectations*

Setting clear expectations rather than operating on assumptions is critical for an organizations' success. Leaders need to let employees know what success looks like.

Setting expectations begins during the interview process. When I interviewed candidates, I would ask what they knew about our organization. The more they knew about it, the better. I wanted them to know the good, the bad, and the ugly parts. We had a good organization, but my expectation was to continue to get better. I looked for people who could solve problems as well as those who could capitalize on opportunities. If they missed critical aspects in their responses, I felt the need to paint a clearer picture of how I saw the organization. It was imperative that any perspective employees fully understand our mission, goals and our method of operation. I would also let them know what they could expect from me.

Setting expectations isn't as simple as it sounds. As an entry level employee, I learned to do my job well. When I was promoted to supervisor, I had two subordinates. One who shared my personality and work style. She was so easy to supervise. I would say "let's" and she would say "go". The other person was vastly different. The more guidance and structure I gave, the more frustrating it became for both of us. I wasn't a micro-manager by nature and that is exactly what I was doing. After a few discussions, I backed off. Rather than mapping out specific processes, I switched from managing day-to-day to managing by the "end game". We agreed on what was to be done and when. I appraised her performance by the results she produced, not by specific tasks and processes. From this experience I learned that the methods the employee chose were different from the way I would approach a situation, but that didn't make it wrong.

Hersey and Blanchard's Situational Leadership theory was very popular around that time. It made the point that one size doesn't fit all when it comes to supervising. While one-size fits all seems easier, it is not as effective as managing/coaching directly based on the individuals' strengths and weakness. In this manner, the expected contribution to the goal will be more effective. In other words, expectations were set based on a common goal, but individual expectations are based on an employee's strengths and abilities.

As I moved up the corporate ladder the lessons learned about expectations setting were extremely valuable when it came to managing supervisors and directors.

## *Goals and Roles*

With a clearer understanding of expectations, it is easier to set goals and determine the contribution each employee will make to the mission. Goal setting comes easy to some people and they enjoy the process. For others it is an unpleasant chore. They have a general idea of what they want to accomplish and intuitively prioritize what needs to be done. These people do not want to be "straight jacketed" by writing things down. Some of them are very successful, especially in small innovative organizations.

I have worked with and without formally set goals. However. I found myself more effective when I took the time to write down my goals. For me, goal setting was like mapping out a trip. This process gave me the opportunity to choose the shortest routes, learn about potential detours, and safely navigate unforeseen conditions.

I started using the SMART Goal approach a few years ago and I found it to be a very thought stimulating planning tool. SMART is an acronym representing criteria for goal setting – S (Specific), M (Measurable), A (Achievable), R (Relevant), T (Timely). It helped to clarify what needed to be done and when. To get desired results, a goal must be specific. Work teams must be clear on what success looks like. The next step is to define how success will be measured. I found it helpful to use the carpenters' rule of measuring twice and cutting once. In other words, employees need to know the standard by which their performance will be measured.

During brainstorming sessions, leadership teams think of a lot of noble and wonderful projects but fail to consider the time frames in which they are to be completed. Many times, they do not consider competing activities. The SMART Goal process forces management to determine if certain endeavors can be achieved in the context of everything else.

The most thought-provoking question that must be answered is: "Why?" In other words, is the endeavor relevant. Group think can stifle a team's creativity and effectiveness. No one wants to be the person to stop the momentum of team members excited about a project. But the "why" question must be answered after critical thought. Although it can be annoying, devil's advocates are necessary. If the project passes the relevancy test, a team can move forward with confidence. We used the SMART Goal approach to complete major projects.

We had to consider each person's capacity to contribute given their overall roles and responsibilities. The SMART Goal approach was essential in helping us accomplish our goals without burning anyone out.

All things considered, a timeline for completion must be set. The timeline must have enough cushion for Murphy's Law; because unexpected things happen.

## SMART Goals

| | |
|---|---|
| **S**pecific | Know exactly what you are wanting to accomplish |
| **M**easurable | How will you know you met your goal? |
| **A**chievable | Make sure your goal is not too far to reach, but far enough to be challenging. |
| **R**elevant | Link the goal to something important to you, something that inspires you. |
| **T**imely | When do you want your goal to be met? |

# Principle 4: Collaborative Exchange

## *Networking*

The Office of Residential Life at Illinois State University had a "three-years up or out" for employment policy. Either you were promoted to a higher position in the department or you'd have to look for a job elsewhere.

I had an opportunity to take a management position at State Farm Insurance Company in the middle of my third year but chose to honor my employment contract. I accepted a commercial underwriter position at State Farm, three weeks after my contract ended.

Six months into my tenure at State Farm, I was asked to apply for a staff position in the Vice President's office at Illinois State University. I chose not to pursue it because my work in corporate America was very rewarding and I was more interested in a line rather than a staff position.

Three months later my former boss at Illinois State University left and I was asked to return as the acting associate director. I informed the Director I would apply for the permanent position, which I did.

After a very competitive and contentious search, I was selected to serve as an associate director there. I was the preferred candidate by the Department Director and many of my former peers. However, I had to make up a lot of ground with the Vice President of the

Division, who perceived my declining previous offers as a snub.

Another challenge was to supervise the people who used to be my peers. I thought the best way to do so was to put my nose to the grindstone and my shoulder to the wheel to prove my competence. Although that was important, the most important thing I needed to do was network and build those relationships. So, my boss and mentor invited me to meetings with the Vice President and Directors. He provided opportunities for me to build relationships with them. He wanted them to know me as he knew me.

The associate director position was two levels higher than the position I left 13 months earlier. Much has been written about networking at events to get to know people in other organizations or with potential employers. I haven't found many examples of how to network in an organization one has returned to. The people I used to commiserate with or discuss how we could do it better than the former boss were now reporting to me. I was their boss.

From my new vantage point, I could see why my predecessor made certain decisions. I felt like those political candidates who could do anything when running for office, but discovered reality after the election.

As a subordinate, I could advocate for things, because I only saw one side of the equation. As the boss, I was responsible for balancing it. Creating new programs cost money and time. If these resources were infinite everything could be done. Hard decisions had to be made. Because I had walked in their shoes, I understood where the former peers were coming from.

My networking took the form of one on one and group discussions. I spent time answering "why" questions and discussing "greater good" decisions. Those conversations helped us become a more cohesive leadership team. And, it paid off by giving them a better understanding of what needs to be considered when making decisions at a higher level. All five of my former peers moved on to higher positions and had stellar careers. We still communicate to this day.

## *Comfort Zone*

Usually everyone who joins a new organization has a honeymoon period. After all, she or he was the preferred candidate. I remember taking a position and wanting to fast forward the clock and have a year under my belt. But, as mentioned in the previous section, getting to know the people at all levels is the important learning endeavor. Building relationships is important for two major reasons: people want to know they matter and they want to be heard. Therefore, I made it a point to get out and mingle with employees who were at different levels in the hierarchy. With over 200 full-time and 600 part-time employees I couldn't meet all of them. So, I strategically set out to meet a representative sample of the employees in each of the 5 major units that comprised the department.

In any organization there are competing priorities that have the potential to cause conflicts. Therefore, I wanted the people in my department to know me on a personal level, not merely as their boss. In addition, I wanted them to know that decisions that didn't go their way were not personal, but for the greater good of the organization.

I had to be careful not to usurp the authority of the unit heads. I welcomed the ideas employees shared with me, but I informed them that all ideas would have to be vetted. I explained that there were few perfect solutions. What solves one problem could create another. In other words, all potential solutions have an up and down side. The ones with the most upside relative to the mission are most likely to be implemented. This approach helped me increase my comfort level with employees and they with me. Everyone felt they would be heard and I promised to give my rationale for any decisions I made.

Some staff felt so comfortable that they would tell me when their peers misbehaved. For example, I happened to be in a video store in the community when a first line employee told me her concern about other employees abusing breaks. She had considered following suit, but with an understanding of the big picture chose not to. She didn't give me the names of the employees but told when and where the abuse was taking place. I informed the unit head and the problem was corrected. That employee took a risk for the good of the organization. If we had not established a comfort zone built on trust, that and similar situations would not have occurred.

Relationships with staff made learning the administrative, procedural, and technical aspects of the position that much easier. After a year, the basic nature of the position was clear. As a department, we stepped out of our operational comfort zone and moved on to bigger and more innovative undertakings.

## *Healthy Competition*

I am opening this segment with definitions that distinguish healthy competition from unhealthy/toxic competition. Competition can be healthy if it makes everyone better as it focuses on performing well and continuously looking for ways to improve. Unhealthy competition focuses on pointing out the flaws of other employees. Toxic behaviors of any kind should be disincentivized at all cost to maintain a healthy organization.

Jack Sands, asks these questions: "What is considered healthy competition? Should we compete against others, ourselves or some common benchmarks? Which way is the best way for an organization to function to achieve its goals?"

According to Amy Rees Anderson, "If you continuously compete with others, you become bitter, but if you continuously compete with yourself you become better."

I agree with her, but there are situations where competing with others can be a rising tide that lifts all boats.

Golf is the best example of how one competes with him/herself and with others at the same time. I was a fair golfer at best but the principles of the game provided lessons for life. I found it required control, focus, physical stamina, emotional stability, and integrity. The more I relaxed and reflected on my inner game, the better I played, whether by myself or with others. These lessons followed me throughout my professional career.

# Section II

# Principle 5: The Other

## *Through the Eyes of the 'Other'*

When I was the director of a large department at Southern Illinois University-Carbondale, each major department rotated sponsorship of the Division's holiday celebration. Each department's turn came up every four years. My Administrative Assistant attended planning sessions in the past therefore she knew the basic agenda and the process. I knew I was going to be late to the first meeting so, I sent her ahead of me to begin. I expected her to start with selecting the speaker, head table seating, and the budget, in no particular order. Based on my experience as a male director, I expected her to start with the selection of speaker, head table seating and/or the budget in no particular order. To my surprise, they were discussing the cranberry salad when I arrived. I realized that the menu was an important aspect of the agenda to them.

Most of the directors were men who wanted structure and order. Most of the people who attended the event were women in clerical positions. They wanted to connect and renew acquaintances. Rather than take the reins of the meeting, I listened to the conversation. At that moment, I saw the event through the eyes of the people it was for. As Directors, we were well intentioned but not serving the staff as well as we could; they had not been included in the decision-making process before. The lesson I learned was this: to be most effective, include the voices and look through the eyes of everyone who has a stake in the outcome.

This was not a controversial situation, but controversy can occur when individuals, especially leaders, look at situations from only one vantage point. Monovision creates "us vs. them" mindsets. Contrary to conventional thought, the bottom line can be enhanced as a result of diverse opinions.

I listened to a video that described a company that lost a lot of market share in a short period of time. The board recommended staff layoffs but the CEO asked for an opportunity to include employees in the decision-making process. Rather than layoffs, employees came up with a plan in which all staff, including executives, would be furloughed for two weeks a year. Some employees furloughed for more than two weeks to allow less fortunate employs to not have to furlough at all. The company saved more money and boosted morale. The result was a win-win-win solution for the board, executives, and employees.

## *Unconscious Bias*

According to psychologists, the unconscious is the part of the mind which is inaccessible to the conscious mind but affects behavior and emotions. Therefore, people do or feel things, but may not know why. I will illustrate this concept with the following story. In preparation for cooking a ham for a Thanksgiving dinner, a mother cut off the ends. Her daughter asked her why she did that.

"I don't know, but my mother always did it," the mother responded.

The girl then asked her grandmother why she cut off the ends of a ham. The grandmother told her that she cut off the ends to fit the ham in to a small pan. The mother was never told to cut off the ends, she did it unconsciously. Her actions were based on what she learned from observing someone else.

Our perspective is a function of our observations and experiences. People tend to gravitate toward those most like themselves. Unfortunately, many peoples' perceptions are formed with the absence of knowledge or pre-programmed by others.

I have been the subject and author of unconscious bias. After working with me for three months, my new boss admitted she was initially intimidated because I was a black male of imposing stature. Everything she'd seen on television and the stories people told her shaped her perspective. But after observing and working with me, she felt obligated to share her misperception. She participated in diversity training but her epiphany came through our association. Although this story ended well, I wondered, had she been the hiring officer, would I have even gotten the chance to prove myself? All of us have unconscious biases. We may not recognize or acknowledge them until we are tested. My former supervisor was tested and so was I. Both of us are better people because of it.

## *Shared Privilege*

When I was growing up my parents told me not to talk with people about politics, their salary, and religion. Those topics can get dicey but race, gender, sexual orientation, national origin, ethnicity, disability, marital status, and social class are just as touchy.

After the high point of the Civil Rights Movement, business and government leaders declared that we were living in a color and gender blind society. Therefore, we didn't need to discuss those issues any longer. We still did some diversity training to satisfy an organizational goal. In many of the sessions I attended, minority group members spoke too much while majority group members said little or nothing at all. They just wanted to get through it without saying anything they'd be taken to task for.

My former boss and lifetime mentor is a straight white male who valued diversity and inclusion. He lived these values among others. He would present on diversity and inclusion topics but his real work was done in dining facilities, sporting events, and street corners. He was told that it was difficult to find qualified African-Americans to fill leadership positions. He held a different opinion, feeling that if given opportunities, people who were different from him could succeed.

He recruited talented and diverse staff throughout his entire career. He reached out to the 'Other', because he had a dream that we were more alike than different and we must acknowledge and respect other cultures.

A lot of people hate the word "privilege" but he was proud of his and was willing to share it. He shared it with me by introducing me to influential people I never would have known and taking me places I didn't know existed. As a straight African-American man, I have male and heterosexual privilege. I share that privilege with women, homosexuals, and others who are less privileged. I do it to pay it forward, because I recognized no single group has a monopoly on talent, and that it is unequivocally right.

# Principle 6: Political Capital

## *Political Capital Exchange*

Whether people know it or not they are either acquiring or losing political capital. Every encounter with bosses, colleagues, subordinates, or clients is an exchange of political capital. The exchange could come in the form of a prepared speech in front of a large audience or a brief conversation around the water cooler.

In the financial world, monetary capital is an exchange of value. That value could be clearly defined when the United States and other nations were tied to the gold standard. Up until the 1970s, every dollar in circulation was associated with a unit of gold or other precious metal stored in a vault. Without a strong connection to gold or other precious metals, a nation or community operates on a fiat currency basis. Fiat currency only has value because parties engaging in the exchange agree that it has value. 'It is the substance of things hoped for and the evidence of things not seen.'

Political capital has a gold standard which is called character or authenticity. According to Stephen Covey, the character ethic is comprised of integrity, humility, fidelity, patience, courage, justice, industry, modesty, and the Golden Rule. The most familiar version of the Golden Rule says, "Do unto others as you would have them do unto to you".

The degree to which trust is present can be traced back to how well these characteristics are woven into the fabric of the organization. It is the stuff of which trust is built on. Trust building takes time, but it is worth it. There are organizations where colleagues talk one way to a person's face and another way when the person is not present. Would you trust a person who did that?

The personality ethic is another useful approach that focuses on public image, attitudes, behaviors, human relations skills, and feel good techniques. It is expedient, but can be ephemeral.

When I was Associate Director of Housing, I interviewed candidates for positions in April. Most used the best of the contents in the personality ethic toolbox. Those skills and techniques were in play in August when they came onboard. However, it was in November and February when their true character showed its face. In November and February, the weather is cold, and the sun doesn't shine as often or long during the day. Students and parents are stressed. The personality ethic alone wouldn't see them through.

With the personality ethic alone, it is difficult to see what lies beneath those surface behaviors. Nevertheless, I won't say that the personality ethic is fiat currency, but its roots do not go as deep as the character ethic. However, used in combination with the character ethic one could weather the storms of work life much better and be a very successful office political operative and amass a great sum of political capital.

## *Lessons Learned*

The character ethic sprinkled with the personality ethic makes the workplace operate at peak performance. We don't live in a perfect world, but there is a standard for which we should strive. I fall short as many of us do. But, my desire is to get a little better every day so I can give myself the best chance for a better outcome.

If you don't like office politics, welcome to the club; you have a lot of company. If you think it can be avoided, you are wrong. If you are engaging the wrong way, I can help you get it right.

Office politics is inevitable and some say it is a necessary evil. I believe it is necessary, but not necessarily evil.

I learned how to create win-win work environments through trial and error. I learned how to survive and thrive in office situations and want to help others do the same. I learned that the key to success in organizational settings is to remain focused on the mission or the "end-game". I will talk about the end-game in more detail in the next chapter.

As a young professional, I entered the world of work with rose colored glasses. My naivete' nearly derailed my career. An entire division witnessed a high-level administrator gain an executive position through dubious means. Morale plummeted. The executive held a division-wide meeting and asked why everyone was so melancholy. I respectfully shared my thoughts. It was not appreciated. With the help of politically savvy professionals, I regained lost political capital.

Fast forward a few years. I have a solid social justice background and am culturally sensitive. Nevertheless, I found myself in an interesting position, at the intersection of social justice and organizational policy. For a variety of reasons only married couples and their children were permitted to live in the department's rent-free apartments.

In 2001 one of my live-in staff members stopped by my office, which was not unusual because of my open-door policy. She informed me that I would be receiving a police report regarding an incident that occurred in her apartment. Her girlfriend had an emotional episode. The staff member stated that her partner had been living there in violation of the agreement live-in staff sign with their employment contract each year. Samantha (not her real name) announced that she wanted her girlfriend to continue living in the apartment. She felt that not allowing her partner to live in the apartment was unfair. She felt the policy was discriminatory because homosexuals could not marry in the state of Illinois. I felt she was violating policy and defying my authority by asking for forgiveness rather than for permission. We had a good personal relationship, so we were able to have a good conversation. I let her know that agreeing to a policy, then violating it, was not a good way to operate.

We agreed that the conversation we were having in the spring should have taken place the previous summer. She informed me that she was going to file a discrimination claim. In response to the claim, the university administration formed a Domestic Partner Policy Committee, put me in charge of it, and loaded it with gay and lesbian faculty and staff. After numerous meetings, we came up with policy recommendations that covered social justice, equity, and liability issues. After our last meetings, I was met by two of the Chancellor's cabinet members. They asked about the recommendations and I was told that as chair of the committee, I should modify the recommendations to something the Chancellor could accept. What would you do?

Well, this is what I did. I submitted the full committee report and recommendations up the chain of command without modification. It sat on the Chancellor's desk for three and half years before it was approved. I shared it with other colleagues in the state and they used it as a template for their Domestic Partner Policies. What started as a conflict turned into an opportunity for a groundbreaking policy change. That's office politics, the right way.

## *Paying it Forward*

In a previous section, I mentioned that political capital is exchanged in a variety of settings. Many of us respond to others based on how they greet us. If a person smiles and says hello, then we'll smile and say hello. If they appear to be non-conversant, then we'll be non-conversant. I can recall an occasion when I found myself in the company of a gentleman whose countenance was hard and fixed. He seemed to be completely closed to any greeting or approach. Rejecting the temptation to reflect the coldness he emanated, I tested the waters and took an emotional risk to speak first. As if coming out of a trance, the person appreciated being acknowledged and responded with a warm reply. You never know what a person is going through. Initiating a greeting could be the thing that brightens their day. If they are committed to being in a bad mood or don't care for you, your self-confidence and inner strength will keep your spirits buoyed. The point I'm making is this; sometimes you've got to pay it forward. It's a law of Karma, what you put out into the world, you'll get back.

Non-verbal communication speaks volumes but could be misread. It's easier to recognize others' non-verbal cues than my own. I recall a morning when everything was going wrong. I had an important meeting that morning, I overslept and was running late, then needed to drop the kids off at school. Since I got a late start, of course traffic was heavier than what I was used to. By the time I got to work I was not in a good mood.

In the grand scheme of things my morning was not that big of a deal, but I was deep in my own world of frustration. A colleague, who was getting coffee, touched me on the shoulder and asked how I was doing. It was as if a reality switch was turned on. After venting my frustration, I became my normal self. I was so glad that person paid it forward because my preoccupation with the events of the morning didn't get in the way of the meeting. Thankfully, the participants didn't get the wrong impression of me.

Taking the first step can make all the difference in the world. At the end of every encounter, ask yourself, "How do I want this person(s) to think and/or feel when the interaction is over?"

To be successful, it is important that people know, like, and trust you. Rather than just wishing and hoping, pay it forward. What you give will come back to you.

# Principle 7: Mission Driven

## *Your Why*

Just about every organization has a mission statement. But, how many leaders, executives, managers, employees, or members know what it says. It is impossible to operationalize a mission statement if you set it and then forget it. Most people know what and how they do things. You can program a robot to do the what, how, and when of an operation, but cannot program the why. The why cannot be programmed because it is emotional.

According to Bill Baren, author of *The Big Shift: the 5 Whys Method*, the more you can get to the real reason people want something, the more likely they are to commit to it. When leaders understand and are deeply committed, they put their heart and soul into a goal and hire the people who will help them get there. Some say that if your why doesn't make you cry, then it has not been revealed to you.

So, how do you find your why? It takes thought and reflection. You were put on this earth to do more than pay bills. You have a purpose or mission in life. When many people are asked the first why, they say to make money. Money is a means to get to your why, but not the purpose. So, a follow up question would be: why do you need the money? The next question would be: why do you want to use the money for that? Another question would be: why is that important to you? The final why question would be: what is your purpose? Once your purpose is revealed to you, it will be easier for you to get out of bed every morning because you will be doing what you were born to do.

With a clear purpose you are ready to write your mission statement. According to Stephen Covey, "Your mission statement becomes your constitution, the solid expression of your vision and values. It becomes the criterion by which you measure everything else in your life." While it contains your purpose, principles, and values, it should also be concise. It should contain key or anchor words that everyone can remember. That way, your audience will know who you are and who you are not. They will also know your why.

## *Your Stake in the Outcome*

It is good to know your why in terms of how you contribute to an organizations mission. If you are there just to collect a paycheck you are in the wrong place.

I was given an assignment as part of the interview process when I applied for an Associate Vice President position at California State University, Sacramento. I had to make a presentation for the search committee. In preparation for that presentation, I picked up a book by Jack Stack called, *A Stake in the Outcome*. I don't know if the concepts in the book helped give me a competitive edge over the other candidates, but it was very helpful to me. One of the key concepts in the book was what the author called an "ownership culture" that was instilled in every employee. An ownership culture is one in which each an every employee believes they have a personal investment in the success of the organization.

I used that concept without knowing it when I collaborated with staff to create our vision, mission, and goals as the Director of Housing and Dining at Southern Illinois University, Carbondale. We started with a SWOT (Strength, Weakness, Opportunities and Threats) analysis which included three tiers of leaders. After thoroughly discussing the results, we collectively charted our courses for the short (one year), intermediate, (five years) and long (15 year) horizons. After the process, the staff was energized because they felt they had a stake in the department's long-term future and they knew their contributions mattered.

Jack Stake discusses two types of ownership cultures: the psychic and the real. The psychic is what I described in the example above. The real is equity in the form of stock. With psychic ownership, employees are more motivated because they are passionate about the mission. Rather than rely on supervisors to keep employees on point, peers and subordinates do it. Transparency is critical here.

Mary Kay cosmetics has an ownership culture. One of my Lyft drivers explained how ownership culture works for them. It is very transparent and very supportive of its associates. It had gone public for a while but the traditional corporate structure was destroying the culture of ownership of the associates. The corporate structure sent most of the earnings to investors. The Mary Kay ownership culture spread the wealth among the associates. The associates preferred to be treated like team members rather than employees.

### *Your Living Mission Statement*

Every organization I have worked for or been a part of had a mission statement. You could tell those written by a committee because they were long and convoluted. I believe many stakeholders should be involved in the process because buy-in is important. However, those involved should understand what a mission statement is and what it is not as well as its key elements.

A mission statement is an organization's identity. It should explain in a simple concise sentence or two the organization's purpose or reason for being in business. It is not a place where every department gets a line to describe who does what. Long mission statements are usually written and forgotten. Unless there is a major upheaval, mission statements don't change. Vision and goal statements may, but not mission statements.

When I arrived at Southern Illinois University, Carbondale, the first document I read was the University Housing and Dining mission statement. Most of the employees knew one existed but couldn't recall what it said, which made it hard to use it as the operational foundation for the department. I was brought in to change the culture and began with the long mission statement. After six workshops over two and a half months, the following mission statement was uncovered:

*University Housing exists to provide a high-quality affordable living/learning environment that contributes to academic success and personal development.*

That mission statement spells out why the department exists and what differentiates it in the marketplace. Using that mission statement as the bedrock for the department, we were able to develop partnerships with Academic Affairs, build new apartments, renovate dining facilities, upgrade menus, and create flexible meal plan options. We used the mission statement to create a marketing and public information unit that developed marketing campaigns and interacted with the media daily. It was easy to remember because all staff had to do was focus on key words when making decisions or speaking with the public: high quality and affordable and living/learning.

# Conclusion

In this book you were exposed to the various aspects of office politics based on my experiences and research. No matter how intelligent or technically skilled, one's career success is built on relationships described in this book. The four relationships that matter most in the workplace are the one with yourself, subordinates, the boss, and colleagues.

The most important relationship is the one I have with myself. After all, how can I help someone if I am not grounded in authenticity? I find it helpful to figuratively look in the mirror to see how my presence and communication style affects others. I also examine my motives to make sure what I intend to communicate is the message the person receives.

I have taken many personality quizzes. One described me as an expressive-driver. As an expressive-driver, I felt people came to work to do their jobs and their personal lives were none of my business. I wasn't harshly demanding, rude, or dismissive. I was open and friendly, but my boundaries, even though unspoken, were there. I called it professional distance. However, my perspective changed when I got sick. Staff went out of their way to support me and my family during that difficult time. While I sought to empower them as employees, they empowered me to be a fully functioning human being. I held babies, attended graduations, weddings, and funerals. Not surprisingly, the personal relationships shifted work relationships into more of a Clan Culture.

I have had eight supervisors over the course of my 35-year career. I am a living witness that the boss can make or break an employee. Most bosses don't ask employees their work styles. Employees must adapt to the supervisors' leadership or management style. I am a self-starting, goal-driven, employee. Give me a target and the appropriate resources and then grade me on the results. I did not like to be micromanaged. I worked best for those who were comfortable with that approach. But at the end of the day, the boss is the boss.

I found relationships with colleagues to be very satisfying. They gave me the opportunity to share ideas, vent frustrations, and offer reciprocal encouragement. In a sense, colleagues at the same level form a mutual support system. The higher the trust the greater the value of peer associations. Professionalism is key because one day, a colleague could become your boss, or you theirs.

The glue that holds everything together is the mission. It is better to have good relationships than bad, but the primary reason you come to work is to serve and/or produce something that consumers need from your organization. Cultivate and nurture relationships and keep your eyes on the prize, that is the mission. That is office politics, the right way.

# References

Bates, B., McGrath, J. (n.d.). Theory 87
Luft and Ingram's Johari Windows. Retrieved
from https://www.oreilly.com/library/view/the-
little-book/9780273785262/html/chapter-
106.html

Brown, B. (2018). *Dare to Lead.* New York, NY:
Penguin Random House, LLC.

Covey, S. R. (1989). *The 7 Habits of Highly Effective
People.* New York, NY: Simon & Schuster, Inc.

Donahue, E. & Harary, K. (1992 , July 2). Who Do
You Think You Are? *Psychology Today.*
Retrieved from
https://www.psychologytoday.com/us/articles/1
99207/who-do-you-think-you-are

Hersey, P., Blanchard, K. (1981). *Situational
Leadership.* Englewood Clift, NJ: Prentice Hall.

Hyacinth, B. (2016, January 16). 4 Kinds of Bad
Bosses that Make Employees Want to Leave.
Retrieved from
https://www.hrmonline.com.au/section/featured
/4-kinds-of-bad-bosses-that-make-employees-
want-to-leave/

Lencioni, P. (2002). *The Five Dysfunctions of a Team.*
San Francisco, CA: Jossey-Bass.

Luft, J., Ingraham, H. (1969). *The Johari Window.* California City, CA: Mayfield Publishing Co.

Morgan, J. (2016, April) Five Signs You're Working for a Truly Great Manager. *Forbes Magazine.* Retrieved from https://www.forbes.com/sites/jacobmorgan/2016/04/26/five-signs-youre-working-for-a-truly-great-manager/#4ba123947e9b

Organizational Culture Types, OCAI Online. (n.d.). Retrieved from https://www.ocai-online.com/about-the-Organizational-Culture-Assessment-Instrument-OCAI/Organizational-Culture-Types

Robin, C. (2011, July 22). What Does it Mean to Be Centered? Retrieved from https://carolrobin.com/what-does-it-mean-to-be-centered/

Stack, J., Birlingham, B. (2002). *A Stake in the Outcome.* Garden City, NY: Altfield Inc.

Veyrat, P. (2016, February 16). Organization Climate Definitions: Everything You Need to Know. Retrieved from www/hello.com/blog/hr/organizational-climate

Wintle, W. (1900). The Man Who Thinks He Can. *Alpha Phi Alpha Membership Handbook.* Retrieved from http://www.alphaforlife.org/Poems.html

Yu, R. K. (2018, March 1). Management Models: The Johari Window. *How can we be more systematic in the ways we see others and others see us in professional interactions?*. Retrieved from https://medium.com/swlh/management-models-the-johari-window-34618f9f3901

www.marykay.com

www.ingramcontent.com/pod-product-compliance
Lightning Source LLC
Chambersburg PA
CBHW072242170526
45158CB00002BA/987